ALFRED'S BEGINNING DRUMSET METHOD

Sandy Feldstein
Dave Black

FOREWORD

Alfred's Beginning Drumset Method is an innovative and practical approach to playing the drumset. You may wish to refer to *Alfred's Drum Method, Book 1* for basic instruction prior to beginning this book.

Students start their first lesson by playing an actual beat! All of the beats and fills presented can be used in a performance situation. The book is divided into two sections—rock and jazz. In each section students learn the use of hi-hat, ride cymbal, snare drum and bass drum technique.

Included with this book is a recording demonstrating many of the beats and fills contained in the book. With the help of the recording, the student is able to hear each of the beats and fills played while following the music. The play-along recording also includes corresponding drum charts (two in a rock style, the other in a jazz style), allowing the drummer to have the experience of actually playing with a group.

The student must set aside a reasonable amount of practice time on a daily basis in order to achieve best results. The authors recommend no less than 30 minutes but some lessons will require more time.

We hope that you will find the book to be an enjoyable experience in your pursuit of musical excellence.

ABOUT THE AUTHORS

Sandy Feldstein is a highly respected performer, composer, arranger, conductor and educator of national prominence. He is the recipient of numerous degrees, including a doctorate from Columbia University, and is an ASCAP award-winning composer. In the area of percussion, Dr. Feldstein has distinguished himself as a leader in percussion education. As past president of the Percussive Arts Society, he was cited by that group for his contribution to the world of percussion. He is a frequent guest lecturer and clinician at universities and music conventions throughout the country. Regarded as a superstar in the educational field, Sandy Feldstein's music and books are used by hundreds of thousands of young people all over the world every day. He is keenly attuned to the needs of the teaching community, and for that reason, has become an innovator in educational music.

Dave Black received his Bachelor of Music degree in percussion performance from California State University, Northridge. He has traveled around the world with a variety of entertainers and shows, performing and/or recording with such artists as Alan King, Robert Merrill, June Allyson, Anita O'Day and Jerry Hey. As a widely published composer/arranger, he has written with and for the bands of Louie Bellson, Sammy Nestico, Bill Watrous, Bobby Shew and Ed Shaughnessy. He is the recipient of eleven ASCAP Popular Composer Awards and two Grammy participation/nomination certificates. He is the co-author of several national best-selling books, including *Alfred's Drum Method, Books 1 & 2, Alfred's Beginning Drumset Method, Contemporary Brush Techniques* and *Cymbals: A Crash Course*. In addition, he has written countless articles, book and concert reviews for such magazines as *Down Beat, The Instrumentalist, Modern Drummer, Jazz Educator's Journal* and others.

The authors wish to thank the following people for their invaluable assistance: Joel Leach, Christopher Leach (model), J. Jeff Leland (photographer), LLoyd McCausland, John O'Reilly and David Tull.

TABLE OF CONTENTS

ARRANGING YOUR DRUMSET

OVERALL SETUP:

The drums and cymbals should be centralized around the player in such a way as to minimize reaching, stretching and twisting. The drums should be set in such a way as to accommodate the player—not the reverse.

THE THRONE (STOOL):

Proper positioning of the throne is very important as it affects the player's balance as well as the ability to use one's feet effectively. Distance from the drums affects reach, while height affects foot movement. One must experiment with both factors until optimum placement is achieved.

THE SNARE DRUM:

Whether played with matched or traditional grip, the snare drum should be positioned and angled in such a way that the proper alignment of the forearms and hands is not affected. With matched grip, the snare drum is usually flat or slanted slightly downward toward the player; with traditional grip, the snare drum is usually tilted slightly downward toward the right (if right handed).

THE MOUNTED (RACK) TOM-TOMS:

Drummers may use one or more mounted toms, which range in size from 10" to 15" in diameter. They should be slightly tilted toward the player in such a way as to allow him/her to clear the drum's rims, while striking the heads comfortably with the side of the stick tip.

THE FLOOR TOM-TOM:

Usually ranging in size from 14" to 16" in diameter, the floor tom should be at approximately the same height as the snare drum. It may be angled slightly toward the player or the snare drum.

THE RIDE CYMBAL:

A ride cymbal is usually 19" to 22" in diameter and medium to heavy in weight. The ride cymbal should be positioned in such a way as to allow the stick to strike 3" to 4" in from the edge.

THE CRASH CYMBAL(S):

Drummers use one or more crash cymbals, which usually range from 16" to 18" in diameter and thin to medium in weight. Crash cymbals should be tilted slightly and positioned within normal reach so that the shaft of the drumstick will strike the edge of the cymbal. Some drummers place their cymbals above normal playing range to maximize visual effects.

THE DRUMSET

Basic Four-Piece Setup

Drumheads

Counterhoop (Rim)

Lug

Shell

Basic Five-Piece Setup

Crash Cymbal

Ride Cymbal

Hi-Hat Cymbals

Mounted Tom-Toms

Cymbal Stand

Cymbal Stand

Snare Drum

Hi-Hat Stand

Floor Tom-Tom

Foot Pedal

Snare Drum Stand

Bass Drum Pedal

Bass Drum

NOTATION

Ride Cymbal w/Stick (R.C.)
Mounted Tom (M.T.)
Snare Drum (S.D.)
Floor Tom (F.T.)
Bass Drum (B.D.)
Hi-Hat w/Foot (H.H.)

GETTING READY TO PLAY

Holding the Sticks

There are several ways to hold drumsticks. Developing the proper position and manner of holding the drumsticks is very important in the development of proper technique, attack and control.

MATCHED GRIP

The Right and Left Hands

The stick should be thought of as a natural extension of the arm. 1) Grip the stick between the thumb and the first joint of the index finger, one-third of the distance from the butt end of the stick. The other fingers will be used to help control the stick. 2) Close the other fingers loosely around the stick. 3) Turn the hand so that the back of the hand is facing upward when playing. The stick should be in line with the wrist and arm.

TRADITIONAL GRIP

The Right Hand

In the right hand, the stick is gripped between the thumb and the first joint of the index finger, one-third of the distance from the butt end of the stick (see matched grip description for details).

The Left Hand

1) Place the stick in the socket between the thumb and first finger, with one-third of the stick (from the butt end) extending behind the hand. The grip should be just tight enough to cause a slight drag if one were to try to pull the stick from the hand. 2) The first two fingers should rest lightly on top of the stick (the first more than the second) to act as a guide. The stick should rest across the third finger, which will act as a support. The fourth finger should rest against the third finger.

STRIKING THE SNARE DRUM

Sound is produced by striking the top head, which sets the air inside the drum in motion, causing the bottom head and, in turn, the snares to vibrate. Best results are obtained when the sticks are allowed to rebound from the head as quickly as possible.

THE STROKE is produced by a turn of the wrist in a down-up motion.

1. Place the tip of the stick on the head.
2. Turn the wrist so the tip of the stick is as far away from the head as possible.
3. Play the stroke (down-up), striking the head and returning immediately to the up position.

When alternating strokes, the right (left) stick strikes the drum and rebounds to a position approximately two inches above the head. When the left (right) stick comes down, the right stick goes from the low position to the full up position.

THE BASS DRUM

The bass drum is usually between 18" and 26" in diameter and. may have one or two heads. It is played with a bass drum pedal operated by the foot.

The bass drum beater is generally made of hard felt or wood.

BASS DRUM PEDAL TENSION ADJUSTMENT

The pedal's spring tension should be adjusted so that when the foot rests on the pedal the beater does not contact the head. The tighter the pedal tension, the faster and stronger the rebound.

Two basic techniques for playing the bass drum are:

1. The entire foot contacts the pedal. The player rocks the foot, causing the beater to strike the head. The foot returns immediately to the "up" position as shown in the diagram. (See diagrams 1a and 1b.)
2. The heel is raised off the pedal surface while the ball of the foot operates the pedal. The foot returns immediately to the "up" position as shown in the diagram. (See diagrams 2a and 2b.)

Usually, the beater should not remain against the head after impact. Rebound technique as discussed earlier applies to all drums.

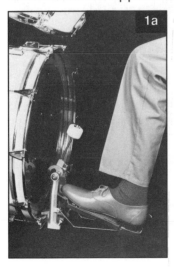

THE HI-HAT

The hi-hat should be placed to the left of the snare drum and operated by the left foot. The hi-hat (sometimes called the "sock cymbal") consists of a pair of cymbals, usually 14" or 15" in diameter, mounted one above the other and connected to a foot pedal. (A good "chick" sound is often achieved by tilting the bottom cymbal slightly.) The most popular combination of hi-hat cymbals is a medium-thin top cymbal and a medium to medium-heavy bottom cymbal.

The space between the cymbals when at rest should be approximately 1" to 2". When the foot pedal is pressed, the cymbals come together.

The top hi-hat cymbal may also be struck by the tip of a drumstick. This may be done while the cymbals are closed, partially closed (cymbals lightly touching) or completely open.

HI-HAT PEDAL TENSION ADJUSTMENT

The hi-hat spring should be tensioned so as to offer strong resistance to the foot when placed on the pedal. The tighter the pedal tension, the faster and stronger the rebound of the pedal.

Two basic techniques for playing the hi-hat are:

1. The "heel-toe" (rocking) technique is often used when playing 2 and 4. In this case, as the ball of the foot presses the pedal down, the heel rises off the pedal, and when the heel goes down, the ball of the foot rises. (See diagrams 1a and 1b.)

2. The "toe" technique is particularly useful when executing rapid rhythms. In this case, the leg is raised to keep the heel off the pedal while the ball of the foot "bounces" up and down to activate the cymbals. (See diagrams 2a and 2b.)

THE RIDE CYMBAL

Cymbals should be mounted on a cymbal stand which has a piece of rubber tubing to serve as a cushion between the stand and the cymbal. The wing nut should never touch the cymbal.

Each ride cymbal has a number of playing areas and each area produces a different sound. When a ride cymbal is struck near the bell, it produces a high pitched "ping" sound (very effective for Latin-American rhythms and funk). When struck near the edge, the cymbal produces a broader sound and more mid-range overtones. About 1/3 of the way between the edge and the bell is generally considered to be the best area for playing the ride-cymbal rhythm.

Other interesting effects can be obtained by using the tip, the shoulder and the butt end of the drumstick on the ride cymbal.

It is very important for the drummer to develop a balance of volume between the ride cymbal, hi-hat cymbals, the bass drum and snare drum. Listen carefully to the blending of all sounds.

ELEMENTS OF MUSIC

WHOLE · HALF · QUARTER NOTES

The duration of musical sounds (long or short) is indicated by different types of notes.

WHOLE NOTE   HALF NOTE   QUARTER NOTE   EIGHTH NOTE   SIXTEENTH NOTE

One whole note equals two half notes.

One half note equals two quarter notes.

One quarter note equals two eighth notes.

One eighth note equals two sixteenth notes.

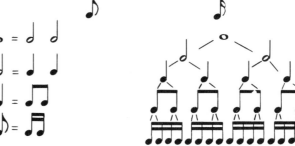

MEASURE · BAR LINES · DOUBLE BAR LINES

Music is divided into equal parts called **MEASURES**.

BAR LINES indicate the beginning and end of measures.

DOUBLE BAR LINES, one thin and one thick, show the end of a piece.

REPEAT SIGNS

Two dots placed before a double bar line ⫶‖ means to go back to the opposite facing sign. If there is no such sign, then go back to the beginning of the music.

TIME SIGNATURES AND NOTE VALUES

TIME SIGNATURES are placed at the beginning of a piece of music. They contain two numbers that show the number of beats (or counts) in each measure and the kind of note that receives one beat.

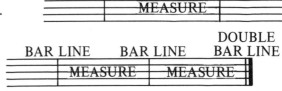

The top number shows the number of beats (or counts) in each measure.
The bottom number shows what kind of note gets one beat.

means four beats in each measure.
means a quarter note (♩) gets one beat.

In 4/4 time, a whole note receives four beats.

A half note receives two beats.

A quarter note receives one beat.

An eighth note receives half of a beat.

A sixteenth note receives a quarter of a beat.

At the beginning of each line of music there is a clef sign. Unpitched percussion music uses the neutral (‖) clef.

TEMPO - The rate of speed of a musical piece or passage. Tempo may be indicated by a musical term or by an exact metronome marking.

METRONOME - A device which produces clicks and/or light flashes to indicate the tempo of the music. For instance, ♩ = 120 means that the metronome will click 120 times in a minute and each click will, in this case, represent a quarter note.

PLAYING ROCK

BASIC ROCK BEATS

Play the following basic beat in which the right hand (on the ride cymbal) and the right foot (on the bass drum) play together.

In many beats, the left hand (snare drum) and the left foot (hi-hat) play together as shown in the following example:

Here's a basic beat that combines the hands and feet. All of the following beats can also be played with the bass drum on 1 and 3 only.

Often, the right stick is played on the hi-hat, which may be partially closed (cymbals lightly touching) or tightly closed. In such cases, the left foot applies light or heavy pressure on the hi-hat pedal.

By changing the right-hand quarter notes to eighth notes, we create a more interesting beat. Beat 5 uses the right hand on the ride cymbal. In beat 6, the right hand moves to the hi-hat.

EMBELLISHING THE LEFT HAND

Eighth notes can also be played by the left hand. Practice all of these beats first with the right hand on the ride cymbal and then on the hi-hat.

The left hand is used to play other drums as well. Beat 4 adds the mounted tom-tom, beats 5 and 6 add the floor tom-tom, while beat 7 incorporates both tom-toms.

EMBELLISHING THE BASS DRUM

So far, the bass drum has played quarter notes on all four beats. Now, we'll change that rhythm somewhat.

After practicing each beat with the the right hand on the hi-hat, repeat them using the right hand on the ride cymbal. (When playing the right hand on the ride cymbal, add the hi-hat on 2 and 4.)

These three bass drum patterns can be used with any of the previous beats. We suggest that you repeat each beat between four and eight times.

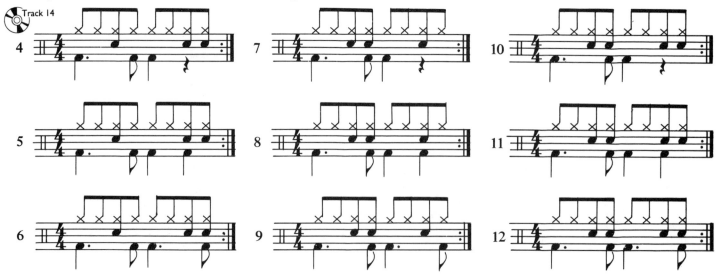

*A dot (.) placed after a note increases its value by one-half the value of the original note.

EMBELLISHING THE LEFT HAND AND BASS DRUM

The dotted quarter- and eighth-note bass drum patterns can also be used with the beats where the left hand moves around the drumset. Practice going across the page (ex. 1, 9, 17, etc.), as well as down the page (ex. 1, 2, 3, 4, etc.), repeating each beat between four and eight times.

Track 15   ♩ = 96

MORE ADVANCED BASS DRUM BEATS

Track 16

Very often the right and left hands remain constant while the bass drum becomes busier. Once you've mastered these beats, you may use your left hand on other drums as shown on page 13. Repeat each beat between four and eight times.

ROCK DRUM FILLS IN CONTEXT

Drum fills are usually played at the end of a musical phrase to serve as a bridge to connect ideas. Always practice fills in a musical "time" setting: we suggest that you play three bars of time followed by the one-bar fill. You may use any of the beats in the previous exercises for the time pattern. Play this page as a complete study, moving from fill to fill (in any order) without stopping. Remember to always play three bars of time between fills. Although fills break away from the basic beat, they should not speed up or slow down.

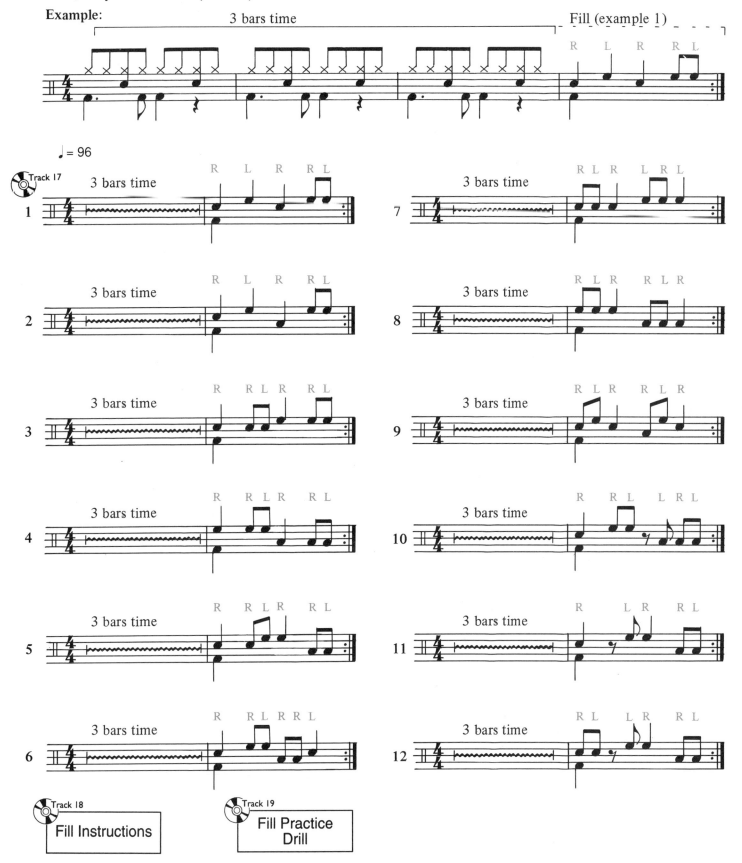

Fill Instructions

Fill Practice Drill

MORE FILLS

Try playing the first note of each bar on the ride cymbal to create an interesting variation. Here are some examples, but you should experiment with your own. Play three bars of time before each fill.

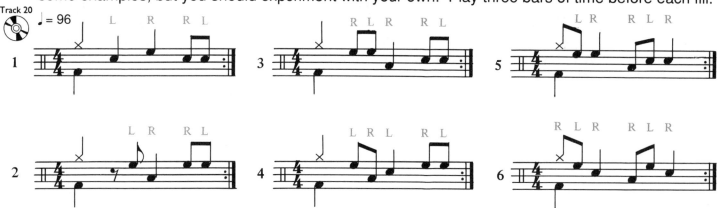

The next group of fills are based on the following sticking patterns:

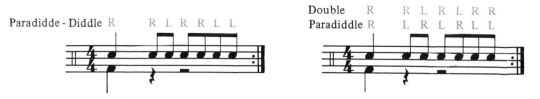

In the rudimental style of snare drumming these are called a paradiddle-diddle and a double para-diddle. Play three bars of time between each fill. Remember, practice across the page (ex. 7, 11, 15, etc.), as well as down the page (ex. 7, 8, 9, etc.).

Track 21

Fill Practice
Drill

TWO-BAR ROCK FILLS

In this section you will play two bars of time followed by a two-bar drum fill. You may use any of the beats in the previous exercises. Play this page as a complete study, moving from fill to fill (in any order) without stopping. Remember to always play two bars of time between fills.

*The flam is a combination of a small note (grace note) and a main note. Its purpose is to produce a broader sound (tenuto).

Track 23
Fill Practice Drill

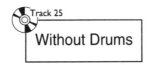
BLUES FOR TIME

The blues is based on a twelve-bar form made up of three four-bar phrases. Many tunes require a fill only in the twelfth bar, but sometimes the music requires fills in bars four and eight as well. After playing the tune as written, try using any of the previous beats and fills that you've learned.

♩ = 130

Comp./Arr. by Gordon Brisker

* ⟮ ∕. ⟯ = repeat the previous bar.

SIXTEENTH-NOTE FILLS

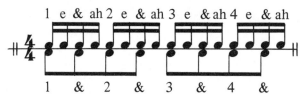

Practice each fill across the page (ex. 1, 7, 2, 8, etc.), as well as down the page (ex. 1, 2, 3, 4, etc.).

Track 27

Fill Practice
Drill

MORE ADVANCED BASS DRUM BEATS

Adding dotted eighth- and sixteenth-note patterns to the bass drum will create some interesting variations.

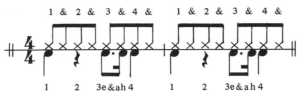

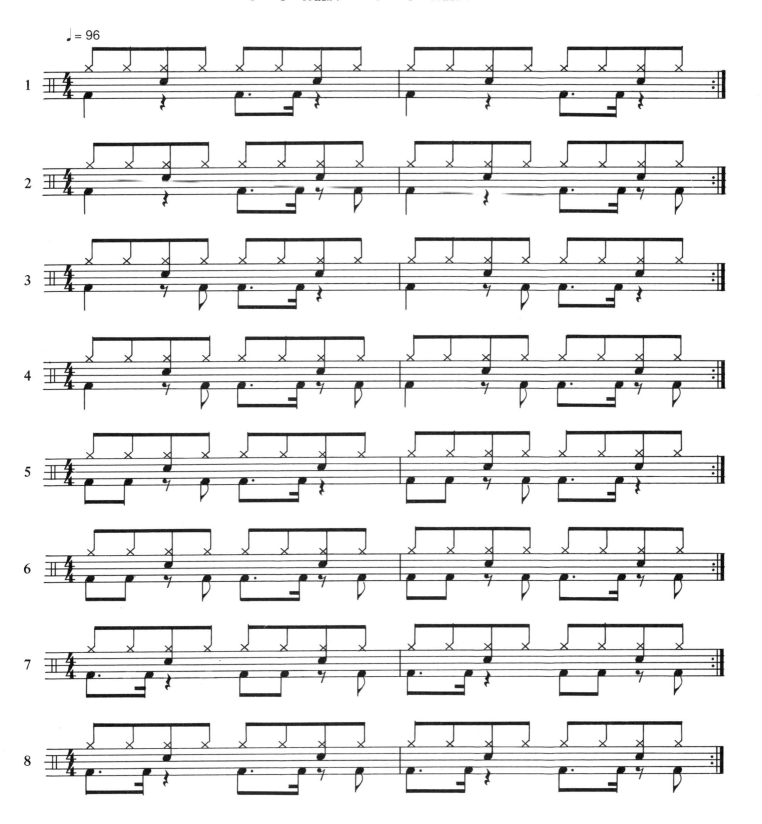

EMBELLISHING THE LEFT HAND

You may also add sixteenth notes to the snare drum and ride cymbal/hi-hat. The bass drum pattern remains constant in beats 1-4 and 5-8.

EMBELLISHING THE HANDS AND FEET

TWO-BAR FILLS USING SIXTEENTH NOTES

In this section you will play two bars of time followed by a two-bar drum fill. As in the previous section, you may use any of the previous beats and should play the page as a complete study, moving from fill to fill without stopping. Although fills break away from the basic beat, they should not speed up or slow down.

Before going on, go back to the chart of *Blues for Time* and play it using the beats and fills that incorporate sixteenth notes.

Track 33
Fill Practice Drill

SIXTEENTH NOTES ON THE HI-HAT

Playing sixteenth notes rather than eighth notes on the hi-hat adds another dimension. If you start the sixteenths with the right hand, the right hand moves to the snare drum on 2 and 4. If you start with the left, the left hand moves to the snare on 2 and 4. Try practicing both ways until you decide which feels best for you. In the following beats, the hands remain the same while the bass drum changes. Play from one to the other in any order.

♩ = 96

R L R L R L R L R L R L R L R L, etc.

MORE ADVANCED SIXTEENTH-NOTE BEATS

In the following beats, the hands become busier while the bass drum pattern remains constant in beats 1-5 and 6-9. If you start with the left hand, all stickings will reverse.

EMBELLISHING THE HANDS AND FEET

MORE ADVANCED FILLS

Remember: 1) Always play three bars of time before each fill. 2) Use different time patterns.
3) Practice the whole page, going from fill to fill (with time between) in any order.

TWO-BAR FILLS INCORPORATING THE BASS DRUM

In this section we have incorporated the bass drum as part of the fill. As in previous sections, you should play two bars of time followed by a two-bar drum fill. You may use any of the previous beats and should play the page as a complete study, moving from fill to fill without stopping.

Track 41
Fill Practice
Drill

WINTER POEM

By Sammy Nestico
Arr. Gordon Brisker

PLAYING JAZZ

BASIC JAZZ BEATS

In rock, the bass drum is of equal importance to the snare drum, but in jazz, the bass drum is used much less frequently and primarily for the purpose of accenting and emphasizing. The basic feel in jazz drumming comes from the cymbals: the "ride rhythm" (played by the right hand on the ride cymbal) and the hi-hat (which most often plays on 2 and 4).

The ride rhythm is based on a triplet feeling as shown in the following example:

Track 44

1   2 (&) ah 3   4 (&) ah, etc.

The ride rhythm pattern is sometimes notated as follows:

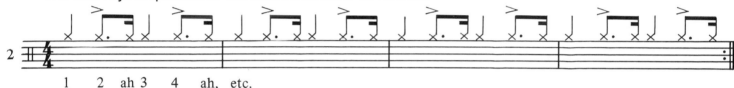

1   2   ah 3   4   ah, etc.

Play the following basic beat in which the ride cymbal and the bass drum play together. The accent (>) on 2 and 4 is very important for the authentic jazz feel. (Beats 1 and 3 should be de-emphasized.)

Practice these exercises with the bass drum on all four beats and then again with the bass drum resting.

Track 45

Track 46 As with rock beats, the left hand (on the snare drum) and the left foot (hi-hat) play together as shown in the following example:

Track 47 Here's a basic beat that combines both hands and both feet.

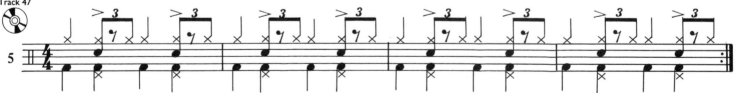

*Use of the bass drum on all four beats in jazz was common practice years ago but is far less common today. For the purpose of this book, the authors decided to show the bass drum playing all four beats so the student would develop balanced coordination. However, once comfortable with that technique, the student should leave the bass drum out when playing basic "time."

Track 48
Example 5 without
Bass Drum

EMBELLISHING THE LEFT HAND

The left hand often plays eighth notes rather than quarter notes on the snare drum as shown in the following beats. As with the right hand, they are played with a triplet feel. Practice these beats with the right hand first on the ride cymbal and then on the hi-hat.

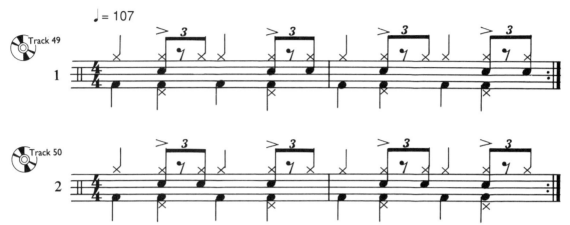

Some of the left hand's notes may be moved to a tom-tom. Beat 3 adds the small (mounted) tom-tom, beat 4 adds the floor tom-tom, while beats 5 and 6 incorporate all of the drums.

PLAYING ON THE HI-HAT

The right hand may also play the ride rhythm on the hi-hat rather than on the ride cymbal. A plus (**+**) sign represents a closed hi-hat, the letter **o** an open hi-hat. When the hi-hat is in the open position, release the foot slightly so that the top cymbal is slightly touching the bottom cymbal.

As with the ride cymbal, the hi-hat rhythm is based on a triplet feeling as shown in the following example:

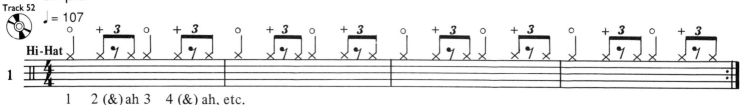

Play the following basic beat in which the hi-hat and the bass drum play together.

Here are some basic beats that combine both hands and both feet. Beats 4-6 are based on a two-bar pattern.

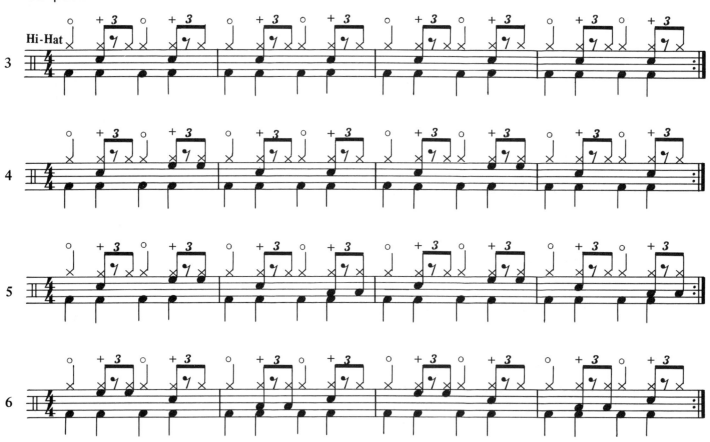

Track 54

LEFT-HAND INDEPENDENCE

LEFT-HAND INDEPENDENCE USING TRIPLETS

Track 55

♩ = 107

JAZZ FILLS

As in rock, jazz fills are usually played at the end of a musical phrase to serve as a bridge to connect ideas. Always practice fills in a musical "time" setting: we suggest that you play three bars of time followed by the fill. You may use any of the beats in the previous exercises. Play this page as a complete study, moving from fill to fill (in any order) without stopping. Remember to always play three bars of time between fills.

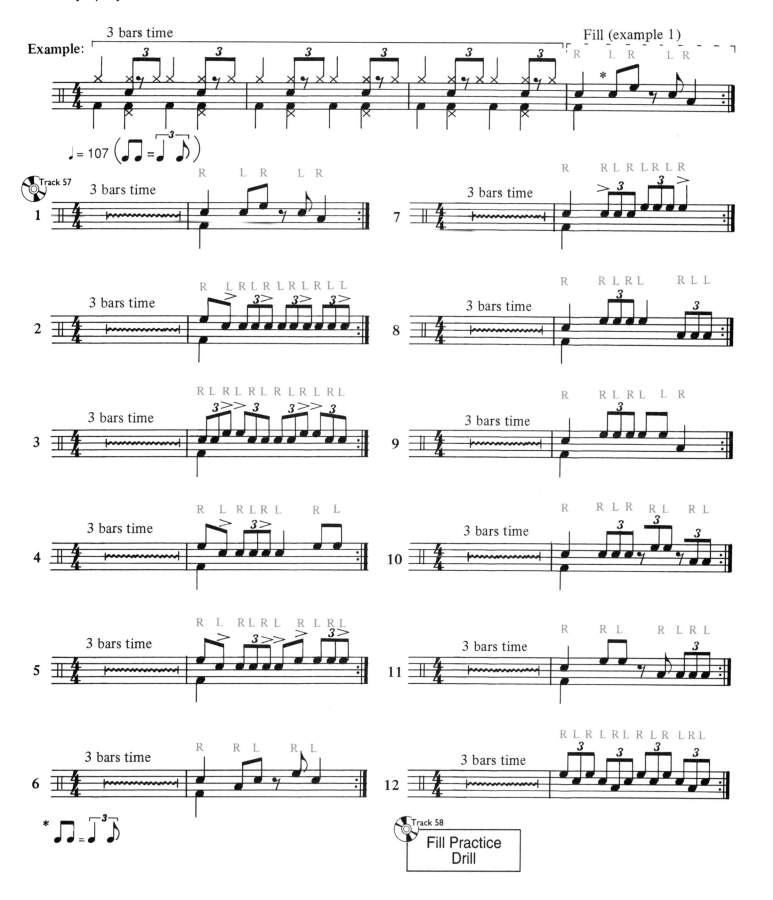

MORE FILLS

To create an interesting variation, play the first note of each bar on the ride cymbal. Here are some examples, but you should experiment with your own. Play three bars of time before each fill.

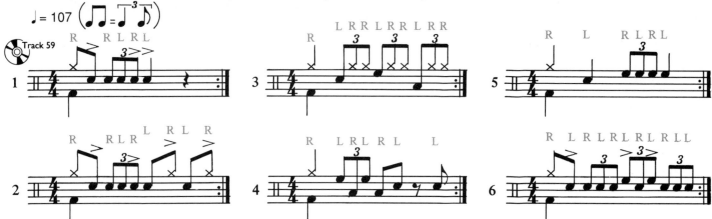

The next group of fills are based on the following sticking pattern:

In the rudimental style of snare drumming this is called a paradiddle-diddle. Play three bars of time between each fill. Remember, practice across the page (ex. 7, 11, 15, etc.), as well as down the page (ex. 7, 8, 9, etc.).

This pattern may also be played with a triplet feel. The first beat can be played on the snare drum or ride cymbal, the second may be a note or a rest.

Track 60

Fill Practice
Drill

TWO-BAR JAZZ FILLS

In this section you will play two bars of time followed by a two-bar drum fill. You may use any of the beats in the previous exercises. Play this page as a complete study, moving from fill to fill (in any order) without stopping. Remember to always play two bars of time between fills.

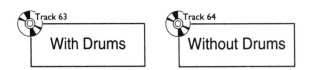

HAVA NICE DAY*

The following tune is in **A-B-A** form, which is one of the most common ways of organizing musical thoughts. The **A** section presents the first musical idea; it is followed by a contrasting **B** section and then the **A** section returns again, although this time the **A** section may be slightly altered.

By Sammy Nestico
Arr. Gordon Brisker

* The big band version, as recorded by Count Basie, may be heard on the album titled *Hava Nice Day* (Daybreak Records, Inc.).

Track 65

BASS DRUM INDEPENDENCE

The left hand, which plays the snare drum, is often used for accents, set-ups and imitation. As a result, it is not used in the following exercises which are devoted to basic time concepts.

SNARE DRUM AND BASS DRUM INDEPENDENCE

JAZZ FILLS UTILIZING
THE BASS DRUM

These fills utilize your right foot as part of the fill. Play three bars of time before each fill using different time patterns. Practice the whole page, going from fill to fill (with time between) in any order.

MORE ADVANCED TWO-BAR FILLS

In this section play two bars of time followed by a two-bar drum fill. You may use any of the beats in the previous exercises. Play this page as a complete study, moving from fill to fill (in any order) without stopping. Remember to always play two bars of time between fills.

*The drag (or 3-stroke ruff) consists of two grace notes and a main note. The two grace notes are played softer than the main note. The drag may begin with either hand.

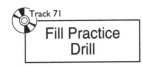

Fill Practice
Drill

APPENDIX

TUNING THE DRUMS

THE SNARE DRUM

The top head of a snare drum is called the batter head; the bottom head is called the snare head. Drumheads are held in place by metal counterhoops, which are adjusted by threaded rods. Tightening or loosening these rods alters the tension of the heads.

When tuning the snare drum the authors suggest that you deal first with the batter head.

Cross-tension system of tensioning

Tune the batter head by using the "cross" method of tensioning, as this maintains even tensioning around the drum throughout the tuning process. Tap the head with a drumstick about two inches from each rod to be certain that the pitch is consistent around the drum. If it is not, adjust individual tension rods as needed.

Clockwise system of tensioning

You may also tune the drum sequentially, moving in a circular fashion around the drum. To begin with, tighten each screw one twist of the wrist until the drumhead feels firm. Be sure not to tension any lug more than the others. Tap the head with a drumstick about two inches in from each rod to be certain that the pitch is consistent around the drum.

The snare head is tensioned in the same manner as the batter head. You may want to use one hand to lift the snares from the surface of the head while tensioning with the other hand to avoid snare rattle as you proceed. Tension the snare firmly, but be sure that it is still able to vibrate freely. Some drummers tighten the batter head tighter than the snare, while others do the reverse. There is no firm rule; it is simply a matter of tone preference.

After achieving the desired pitch and tension for both heads, tap the batter head with a drumstick while adjusting the "snare adjustment screw" to bring the snares into contact with the head and to achieve the desired sound. Be careful not to overtighten the drumheads or the snares, as you will "choke" the drum's sound. Test repeatedly by striking the heads with a drumstick while making adjustments.

THE SNARES

Wire snares are most commonly used on concert and kit drums. They have an excellent sound, are not affected by weather conditions and require little upkeep.

Gut snares are more often used on marching drums, where a crisp sound and a high volume level are required. Since gut snares are affected by humidity, extra care is required to maintain them.

THE BASS DRUM AND TOM-TOMS

It's important that the tension be equalized around the entire circumference of the bass drum and tom-toms to obtain the best tone. This is accomplished in the same manner as when tuning the snare drum.

The tone of the bass drum should be "dark" and low in pitch. If the head is too loose, it will vibrate lifelessly; if too tight, it will ring too much. Both heads should be at approximately the same pitch for maximum resonance. The multiple tom-toms of varied diameters should be tensioned to sound high to low as one moves from left to right.

DRUMHEAD SELECTION

Whereas drumheads were once traditionally made of animal skin, it is far more common today to use heads made of plastic. There are numerous brands and thicknesses of plastic heads on the market today, so the drummer will have to choose wisely those that best fit his/her needs.

Plastic heads become soiled after continued use and may be cleaned with a damp cloth and mild soap or cleanser.

MUFFLING

For muffling the drums sound and controlling "afterring," the authors recommend "Remo Muff'ls" rather than taping drum heads and stuffing drum shells with pillows. Muff'ls fit inside the drum without attachment and provide three stages of sound modification: moderate ring control, studio muffling and silent practice.

MAINTAINING DRUMS

Regular cleaning of your drums will help prolong both their beauty and tone. Wood and pearl finishes may be cleaned with a damp cloth and mild soap; furniture polish may also be applied to wood finishes if desired. Metal shells and hoops may be cleaned with a damp cloth and/or metal polish.

Tension rods should be lubricated with Vaseline or light grease. Moving parts, including the snare throw-off switch, bass drum pedal and hi-hat pedal, should be lubricated with light machine oil.

The safest and easiest way of cleaning your cymbals is to use Comet cleanser, Brasso or some other nonabrasive cleanser. Never use steel wool or any other abrasive material. Most cymbal manufacturers market specially formulated cymbal cleaning products.

STUDENT'S PRACTICE RECORD

To become a good musician you must practice every day. Find a convenient place where you can keep your instrument, book, music stand and any other practice equipment. Try to practice at the same time every day. To help you schedule your time, use this Daily Practice Record.

Name _____   Band Class (Day/Time) _____

Date	Lesson Assignment	Mon.	Tues.	Wed.	Thurs.	Fri.	Sat.	Sun.	Approved